# Stay Safe Online

LEVEL 6

/a_e/ay/
/i_e/

DECODABLES BY jump!

# Teaching Tips

## Orange Level 6

This book focuses on the phonemes **/a_e/ay/i_e/**.

## Before Reading

- Discuss the title. Ask readers what they think the book will be about. Have them briefly explain why.
- Ask readers to say the name of each object on page 3. Which ones end in i_e? What letters and sounds do the names of the other objects end in?

## Read the Book

- Encourage readers to break down unfamiliar words into units of sound. Then, ask them to string the sounds together to create the words.
- Urge readers to point out when the focused phonics phonemes appear in the text.

## After Reading

- Encourage children to reread the book independently or with a friend.
- Ask readers to name other words /a_e/, /ay/, or /i_e/ phonemes. On a separate sheet of paper, have them write the words.


5357 Penn Avenue South
Minneapolis, MN 55419
www.jumplibrary.com

Decodables by Jump! are published by Jump! Library.


Library of Congress Cataloging-in-Publication Data is available at www.loc.gov or upon request from the publisher.

ISBN: 979-8-88524-760-3 (hardcover)
ISBN: 979-8-88524-761-0 (paperback)
ISBN: 979-8-88524-762-7 (ebook)

**Photo Credits**

Images are courtesy of Shutterstock.com. With thanks to Getty Images, Thinkstock Photo and iStockphoto. Cover – AJP, p2–3 – CapturePB, FabrikaSimf, Kateryna998, Mega Pixel, Mindscape, Pixel-Shot, Regreto, vector. p4–5 – ESB Professional, CreativeAngela, p6–7 – Martin Vorel, PHOTOBUAY, p8–9 – LightField Studios, Ground Picture, p10–11 – Milano Art, Monkey Business Images, Rawpixel.com, p12–13 – Marcos Mesa Sam Wordley, monkeybusinessimages, p14–15 –Lucky Business, myboys.me, p16 – Shutterstock.

Point to the pictures that have i_e in their name.

When we are on the internet, we say that we are online. It is important that we stay safe when we are online.

Lots of people like the internet. There is lots to see and do. People across the planet can all be online at the same time.

We can play games with lots of people online. We can dive into a car chase or a tennis match.

We can chat with lots of people too. We can invite friends to chat on lots of internet websites.

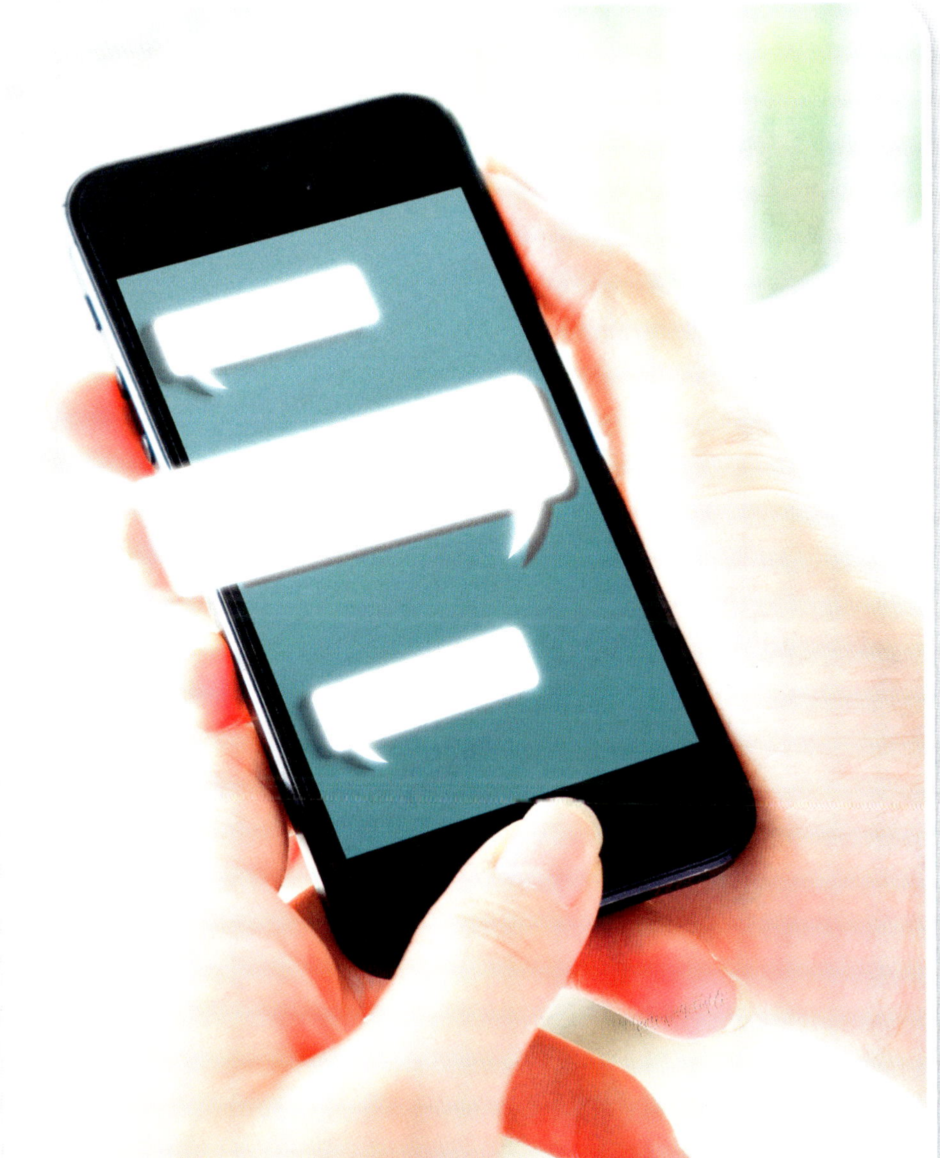

But we must be safe when we are online so that we do not get into problems.

Some people do not behave in the same way when they are online. They may not be the same as they are in real life.

Some people may say mean things when they are online. It is important to talk to an adult if someone upsets you.

Some websites are not made for kids. Speak to an adult to ask which websites you can visit so they can make sure things are safe.

We can chat with lots of people online. But not all people on the internet are the same person they say they are.

Never agree to meet people you chat with online. Always make sure you speak to an adult that you trust if someone asks to meet you.

You do need to be safe online, but you do not need to hide from the internet.

Lots of websites are good and filled with fun things to make us smile. We can all enjoy the internet, as long as we stay safe.

Can you name the missing letters for each word?

c__k__

spr____

d__v__